SPICES COLLECTION

DISCOVER THE BEST HOMEMADE SEASONING BLENDS

SARAH MILLER

CONTENTS

Introduction   v

1. Spices   1

Conclusion   41

INTRODUCTION

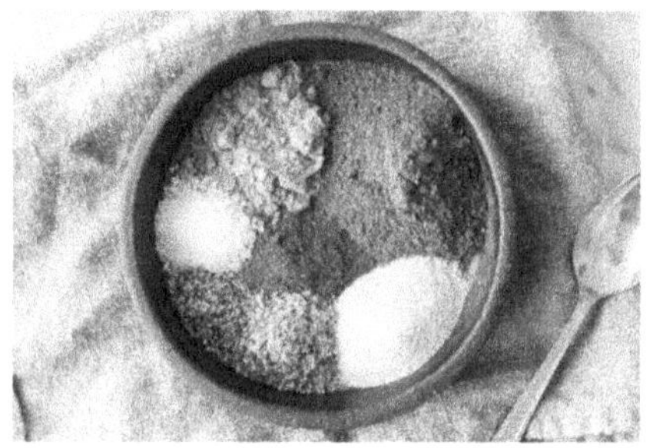

Spices are the highlight of any truly distinctive cooking. Spices give extraordinary flavor to your foods. Apart from contributing a rich and exceptional taste to your foods, spices can also help to improve your general health. Most of the spices examined in this book have ancient origins and were utilized not only for the incredible taste they added to foods but for the important roles they played in the proper and excellent functioning of the human body.

Much like fruits and vegetables, due to their rich components, spices have been found to act as antioxidants, helping to counter-act oxidative processes in the body, thereby slowing down the aging process and improving the integrity of vital internal and external organs. Spices have also been reputed to have superb anti-inflammatory capabilities, making them brilliant in fighting against several disorders of the gastrointestinal tract such as enteritis. A lot of spices also possess potent antibacterial and antiviral properties. These characteristics of spices make them perfect food additives for the eradication of unwanted pathogens from the body system. As humans, we are constantly exposed to harmful microorganisms in the environment. Dusty terrains and extreme weather conditions may escalate the quantities of microorganisms in the environment, making the incorporation of microbes into our body systems almost inevitable. Eating spice-filled foods may go a long way in helping to establish a favorable bacterial balance in your body.

Spices have also been reported to help to manage weight and prevent cardiovascular diseases in the long run, if consumed in the right quantities. Therefore, spices need to be an important part of your diet to help you prepare delicious and nutritious foods. In this book, 30 exciting and medicinal spices would be reviewed, and step-by-step processes to creating each spice from the comfort of your home would be described. This book is literally ready to take you by the hand and take you on a journey to creating spectacular meals packed with highs nutritious value. So, sit back, enjoy, and then practice!

SPICES

The Berbere Spice Mix

Berbere is a bright-orange spice mix of Ethiopian origin. The North African spice mix incorporates varying quantities of several common and individually exciting spices such as paprika, cayenne pepper, ginger, cumin, and coriander to give a single unique blend that casts an exceptionally unique taste into every food it is used for.

The Berbere spice mix can be used for a wide variety of foods, from chicken and pork to pies and French fries.

Total Cooking Time: 32 minutes.

Serving Size: 1 cup

Ingredients:

- ½ cup dried, powdered New Mexico Chili
- ¼ cup paprika
- 1 tbsp Cayenne Pepper
- 1 tsp Onion powder
- 1 tsp ground ginger
- 1 tsp cumin
- 1 tsp powdered coriander
- ½ tsp powdered garlic
- 1 tsp powdered fenugreek
- 1 tsp powdered cardamom
- ½ tsp powdered allspice
- ½ tsp powdered cloves
- ¼ tsp powdered nutmeg
- ½ tsp milled cinnamon

Instructions:

1. First, add the powdered chili, cayenne pepper and paprika into a bowl, and stir thoroughly.

2. Then, add in your onion powder, ginger, allspice, cloves, nutmeg cinnamon, powdered garlic, fenugreek, cardamom, coriander and cumin to the already prepared mixture in the bowl.

3. Carefully but firmly, whip all the ingredients in the bowl together until all the ingredients are fully blended. Fine

bright-orange powder with a fine consistency should be achieved.

4. The final Berbere mix may then be stored in a firmly closed airtight container and used for a wide variety of meals.

Chinese Five-Spice Powder

As deducible from its name, the five-spice powder has its roots in ancient China, where it has been in use for centuries in the making of exceptional Chinese delicacies. For today's mode of meals, the five-spice powder can easily be incorporated into noodles, chicken wings, grilled BBQ, pork, and even rice. It all depends on the taste you want to achieve and how far you can let your imaginations run.

The brown and slightly gritty powder confers a unique and vintage taste to your cooking, and its rich ingredients give this awesome blend of incredible health benefits.

Total Cooking Time: 10 minutes

Serving Size: 1/3 cup

Ingredients:

- 1 tsp powdered cinnamon

- 1 tsp crushed anise seeds
- ¼ tsp crushed fennel seeds
- ¼ tsp powdered fresh pepper
- 1/8 tsp powdered cloves

Instructions:

1. Gather your ground cinnamon, anise seeds, fennel seeds, fresh pepper and cloves in a bowl.

2. Mix thoroughly until a fine, homogenous blend is achieved.

3. Keep your spice mix in an airtight container. The result of this recipe gives 3 teaspoons of the Chinese five-spice powder.

Khmeli-Suneli

This fantastic spice mix from Georgia is a true treasure to behold. Traditionally used in Georgia to confer a specific, unique flavor to the native kharchio stew, which is a thick soup made using beef and chicken, khmeli-suneli has found its place in the kitchens and hearts of many food enthusiasts who have fallen in love with the magnificent flavor of the blend. The spice blend incorporates a lot of local spices and gives your food a brilliant, inimitable taste.

Total Cooking Time: 5 minutes

Total Serving Size: 14 Tbsp

Ingredients:

- 2 tbsp dried summer savory
- 1 tbsp dried fenugreek leaves
- 2 tbsp crushed coriander
- 2 tbsp dried mint
- 2 tbsp dry marjoram
- 2 tsp dried and crushed marigold petals
- 2 tbsp dried dill
- 1 tsp ground black pepper
- 2 tbsp dried parsley
- 1 tsp crushed fenugreek seeds
- 2 pcs ground bay leaves

Instructions:

1. Simply combine all the ingredients listed, in the right proportions in a ceramic or glass bowl.

2. Mix all the ingredients together, firmly but gently until a fine, even consistency is achieved.

3. Store your spice mix in an airtight container. This recipe makes 1 cup of Khmeli-Suneli.

Curry Powder

Curry powder is a versatile and extremely popular spice that is used for thousands of dishes all over the world. Perfect for stews, sauces, and dishes of all kinds, this light brown spice has a way of adding a touch of magical flavor to every single meal it is used for. Curry may also be used for frying chicken, pork, and beef, and has been found to contain essential minerals such as sodium, potassium, calcium, and Iron. Curry is also a rich source of Vitamins A and C.

Total Cooking Time: 5 minutes
Total Serving Size: 1/3 cup
Ingredients:

- 2 tbsp powdered coriander
- 2 tbsp powdered cumin
- 1½ tbsp powdered turmeric
- 2 tsp powdered ginger
- 1 tsp dried mustard
- ½ tsp crushed black pepper
- 1 tsp powdered cinnamon
- ½ tsp crushed cardamom

- ½ tsp ground cayenne pepper

Instructions:

1. Assemble all collected spices into a small bowl.

2. Stir thoroughly until an even consistency is achieved.

3. Pour the curry powder into a small glass or ceramic jar.

4. Shake thoroughly to ensure homogeneity.

5. Store in the airtight jar. Curry powder can be preserved, if kept away from air and moisture, for up to three months.

Chili Powder

Chili is another globally-renowned and unique-tasting spice with a history just as rich as its magnificent taste. Chili powder has been traditionally used to make popular chili dishes for hundreds of years, and the ubiquitous spice is also indispensable in the creation of any type of sauce at all – chicken, beef, mutton, and even ham. Chili powder can easily be created from its constituent elements within 5 minutes and contains a rich array of minerals, including sodium, potassium, calcium, and iron.

Total Cooking Time: 5 minutes

Serving Size: 1/3 cup

Ingredients:

- 1/8 cup Sweet paprika
- ½ tsp smoked paprika (optional)
- 1½ tsp grounded garlic
- ½ tsp grounded cayenne pepper
- 1½ grounded onion spice
- 1 tsp dried oregano
- 1 tsp milled cumin

Instructions:

1. Add all ingredients into ceramic or glass bowl.

2. Mix gently but thoroughly until an even, fine consistency is achieved.

3. Store the mixture in an airtight container. This incredible homemade spice may be stored for up to a year if kept away from air and moisture.

Za'atar

The Za'atar spice mix is a fantastic blend of exotic and

local spices that can be used for a ton of cooking applications. This spice, which is of Middle Eastern origin, may be used as a rub for chicken, fish, and beef, and combines perfectly with olive oil to produce an exotic-tasting marinade.

Total Cooking Time: 5 minutes
Serving Size: ½ cup
Ingredients:

- 1 tbsp crushed thyme
- 1 tbsp Powdered cumin
- 1 tbsp Powdered coriander
- 1 tbsp Heated and ground sesame seeds
- 1 tbsp Sumac
- ½ tsp Kosher salt
- ¼ tsp Aleppo chili flakes (optional)

Instructions:

1. Heat whole sesame, coriander and cumin seeds if the whole seeds are available. If they are not, then powdered spices may be used instead.

2. Assemble listed ingredients in a small glass or ceramic bowl.

3. Mix the spices thoroughly until a fine, even consistency is achieved.

4. Store in an airtight jar.

Kansas City Dry Rub

This spice mix from the sunny city of Kansas has been in use for decades as an ever-reliable and unique rub for Barbecued pork ribs. The dry rub can, however, also be used to spice up your chicken, beef, and pork chops. The Kansas City dry rub is a highly versatile blend that would add an edgy tinge of excitement to every single meal.

Total Cooking Time: 40 minutes

Serving Size: 12 servings

Ingredients:

- ¼ cup paprika
- ½ cup brown sugar
- 1 tbsp black pepper
- 1 tbsp powdered cayenne pepper
- 1 tbsp ground garlic
- 1 tbsp chili powder
- 1 tbsp ground onions
- 1 tbsp table salt

Instructions:

1. Assemble all ingredients in a small glass or ceramic bowl.

2. Mix all constituent spices thoroughly until a homogenous mixture is gotten

3. Store the resultant mixture in an airtight jar away from moisture.

Gomasio

Gomasio is a Japanese spice mix reputable for its distinctive taste and its healing properties. It is probably one of the easiest spice mixes of all time to make, and it confers an unmistakably delicious taste to all foods it is used for. The Gomasio blend contains proteins, fiber, and calcium, and tastes even better when prepared fresh at home, instead of buying in stores.

Cooking Time: 20 minutes

Serving Size: 32 servings

Ingredients:

- 1 tbsp Celtic sea salt
- 2 cups whole sesame seeds

Instructions:

1. Using a cast-iron skillet, roast your whole sesame seeds over medium heat for 10 minutes.

2. Pour your roast sesame seeds into a mortar and add the Celtic salt.

3. Pound the mixture of the sesame seeds and the salt in the mortar until an even, fine consistency is achieved.

4. Pour the spice mix into an airtight glass jar, and store for up to 3 weeks, preferably in a refrigerator.

Togarashi

This fantastic spice mix of Japanese origin has warmed its way into hearts and homes since the 17th century and has remained an indelible component of Japanese cuisine ever since. Togarashi is made from seven unique constituent spices and confers a deliciously enticing flavor to foods from different kinds – from noodles to grilled chicken and pork to stews and soups. Whatever dish you are trying to create, the Togarashi spice blend promises to make it extraordinary.

Cooking Time : 10 minutes

Serving Size: 1 cup

Ingredients:

- 2 tbsp red Chili Powder
- 1 tbsp dried and crushed orange peels
- 2 tsp ground white sesame seeds
- 2 tsp ground black sesame seeds
- 1 tsp Sichuan or Sancho peppercorns
- 1 tsp grounded ginger
- ½ tsp crushed poppy seeds
- ½ sheet crumbled toasted nori

Instructions:

1. Assemble the white and black sesame seeds, the Sichuan or Sancho peppercorns, and the whole poppy seeds in a dry skillet, and heat gently until they become fragrant.

2. Transfer the heated ingredients to a grinder and pulse them gently until a coarse consistency is achieved.

3. Store your coarse spice mix in a sealed glass or ceramic jar away from air or moisture. For best results, the Togarashi spice should be used within three weeks of preparation.

Herbes De Provence

Herbes de Provence is one of the finest and most remarkable spice blends in the world. Originally first prepared in

Southern France, this fantastic blend of herbs has warmed its way into every culture of the world with its exceptional taste and its distinctive smell. The Herbes de Provence can be added to foods while cooking and can also serve as a fantastic rub for poultry meat, beef, and pork.

Total Cooking Time: 5 minutes

Serving Size: 11 tablespoons

Ingredients:

- 2 tbsp dried savory
- 3 tbsp dried thyme
- 2 tbsp powdered oregano
- 2 tbsp dried parsley
- 1 tbsp dried rosemary
- 1 tbsp dried marjoram
- 1 tbsp dried lavender flowers

Instructions:

1. All constituent spices are to be assembled in a bowl and mixed gently but thoroughly.

2. To achieve a finer consistency, the mix of herbs may be grounded using a grinder or a mortar and pestle.

3. The spice blend may then be stored in an airtight container.

Cajun Seasoning Blend

The homemade version of the infamous Cajun spice mix gives a stronger and more distinctive flavor than the ones on the shelves, and the absence of preservatives and filters makes it a lot healthier. The Cajun seasoning blend is a fantastic additive for pasta, rice, and noodles, and can be used as a tangy rub for various types of meat.

Cooking Time: 10 minutes

Serving Size: 7 - 8 tbsp

Ingredients:

- 2½ tbsp sea salt
- 1 tbsp oregano
- 1 tbsp paprika
- 1 tbsp cayenne pepper
- 1 tbsp black pepper
- 1 tsp onion powder
- 1 tsp garlic powder

Instructions:

1. Assemble all listed ingredients into a glass or ceramic bowl.

2. Stir all the ingredients together thoroughly until an even, fine consistency is achieved.

3. Store the spice blend in an airtight jar.

Jerk Seasoning Blend

Jerk seasoning blend is a brilliant combination of several individually spectacular spices and has was first used as a unified seasoning mix in the Caribbean islands. The jerk seasoning blend has a touch of exotic splendor to every single meal and can be used for a variety of soups, stews, and meats.

Total Cooking Time: 10 minutes
Serving Size: 7 - 8 tbsp
Ingredient:

- 3 tbsp dried minced onions
- 1 tbsp thyme
- 1 tbsp allspice
- 1 tbsp black pepper

- 1 tsp cinnamon
- 1 tsp cayenne pepper
- ½ tsp sea salt
- 1 tsp garlic powder

Instructions:

1. Assemble all listed ingredients into a glass or ceramic bowl.

2. Whisk all the ingredients together thoroughly until an even, fine consistency is achieved.

3. Store the spice blend in an airtight jar.

Mediterranean Seasoning Blend

As depicted by the name, this unique spice mix originates from the Mediterranean countries of Turkey and Greece but features a touch of Italian brilliance. This spice blend confers such a delicately exotic feel to every meal that has become an integral part of most American kitchens for decades. The Mediterranean seasoning blend goes well with meat, poultry, fish, and vegetable-based dishes.

Total Cooking Time: 10 minutes

Serving Size: 7 - 8 tbsp

Ingredients:

- 2 tbsp basil
- 2 tbsp oregano
- 2 tbsp kosher salt
- 1 tbsp parsley flakes
- 1 tbsp dried onions
- 1 tsp black pepper

Instructions:

1. Pour your basil, kosher salt, dried oregano, parsley flakes, dried onions and black pepper into a glass or ceramic bowl.

2. Using a whisk, mix all spices thoroughly until a fine, homogenous mixture is attained.

3. Carefully transfer the spices into an airtight jar, and store in a cool, dry place.

Salt-Free All-Purpose Seasoning Blend

This seasoning blend is most remarkable for its healthiness. If you are looking to add a touch of sumptuous flavor to your food without spiking your body's sodium levels, then this simple yet delectable seasoning mix is the right fit for you. This seasoning blend is perfect for vegetables, meat, and even baking pastries.

Total Cooking Time: 10 minutes

Serving Size: 7 - 8 tbsp

Ingredients:

- 2 tbsp grounded garlic
- 2 tbsp onion powder
- 1 tbsp grounded chili
- 1 tbsp paprika
- 1 tbsp parsley
- 1½ tsp black pepper

Instructions:

1. Pour all the ingredients into a glass or ceramic bowl.

2. Mix the ingredients with a ladle until you get an even consistency.

3. Transfer into an airtight jar and store.

Ranch Seasoning Blend

This homemade blend is a brilliant, healthier, and way more affordable alternative to the expensive ranch seasoning mix packets sold at grocery stores. The ranch seasoning blend is brilliant for making spectacular proteins – chicken, beef, ham, and even fish, and costs only a fraction of the price of an industrially-manufactured ranch seasoning mix.

Total Cooking Time: 10 minutes
Total Serving Size: 7 - 8 tbsp
Ingredients:

- 2½ tbsp parsley
- 2 tsp grounded dill
- 2½ tsp grounded garlic
- 2½ tsp onion powder
- 2 tsp dried onions
- 1 tsp black pepper
- 1½ tsp sea salt

Instructions:

1. Find a glass or ceramic bowl and dump the ingredients into it.

2. Stir consistently until you have a fine mixture.

3. Pour the spice blend into a jar and store. Keep covered.

Homemade Poultry Seasoning Mix

This superb homemade poultry spice mix is affordable, easy to make, and perfect for the preparation of all types of poultry – turkey, chicken, duck, and even pheasants. It's also suitable for use in stuffing, gravy, sauces, and meatloaves. Its use is, however, not limited to only poultry meat – it is also perfect for pork and ham chops. This homemade poultry seasoning mix contains Potassium, Vitamin A, and Vitamin C, making it not only delightful to the taste but also quite healthy.

Total Cooking Time: 5 minutes
Serving Size: 6 tbsp
Ingredients:

- 2 tbsp powdered sage
- 1½ tbsp thyme
- 1 tbsp Marjoram
- 1 tbsp rosemary
- ½ tbsp nutmeg
- ½ tbsp black pepper

Instructions:

1. Gather your ingredients and pour them inside a glass or ceramic bowl.

2. Mix together gently until you have a fine mixture.

3. Find an airtight jar and transfer the mixture into it.

Italian Seasoning Blend

First used in the royal castles of Italy, the Italian seasoning blend has quickly spread all over the globe courtesy of its fantastic flavor and its great versatility. The Italian spice mix can be used for a variety of foods – soups, stews, and meats. The Italian seasoning blend is also very easy to make and is highly affordable.

Total Cooking Time: 10 minutes

Total Serving Size: 7 - 8 tbsp

Ingredients:

- 4 tsp basil
- 4 tsp oregano
- 4 tsp rosemary
- 4 tsp marjoram
- 4 tsp thyme
- 4 tsp savory

- 2 tsp grounded garlic

Instructions:

1. The first thing to do is to get your ingredients ready. Now, get a glass or ceramic bowl and pour the ingredients inside.

2. Stir together to achieve an even consistency.

3. You are done. Get them into an airtight container or jar and store.

Taco and Fajita Seasoning Blend

You don't always have to buy the expensive packaged Taco and Fajita seasoning mix available stores, you can opt to have some fun getting your hands dirty, and still, save a few bucks by making your own spice mix in the comfort of your kitchen. This unique seasoning blend has its roots in South America and is hence perfect for all Mexican and Southwestern-themed dishes. The condiments are relatively easy to source, and the process is just as delightful as the amazing taste of the Taco and Fajita seasoning blend. This spice mix is perfect for tacos, casseroles, chili, and even meats, and it has a low sodium content making it perfect for individuals conscious about their salt intakes.

Total Cooking Time: 10 minutes

Serving Size: 7 - 8 tbsp

Ingredients:

- 2 tsp grounded chili
- 2 tsp coriander
- 4 tsp cumin
- 1 tsp grounded onions
- 1 tsp grounded garlic
- 1 tsp oregano
- 2 tsp sea salt
- 1 tsp smoked paprika
- ½ tsp grounded black pepper
- ¼ tsp grounded chipotle chili

Instructions:

1. Collect the ingredients and pour them into a bowl.

2. Mix together thoroughly until you get a fine blend.

3. Transfer the mix into a container and keep tightly covered. Store in a cool and dry place.

Pumpkin Spice Mix

This brilliant yet affordable blend of spices is a true marvel to behold. The pumpkin spice is quite unique because it can be used for a wide range of dishes, from being added to the filling for apple pie, to being incorporated into whipped cream to give a beautifully matchless taste. The pumpkin spice mix is also extremely practicable because each spice can be used individually for cooking a wide range of dishes.

Total Cooking Time: 5 minutes
Serving Size: 6 tbsp
Ingredients:

- 3 tbsp cinnamon
- 2 tbsp powdered ginger
- 1 tsp ground allspice
- 1 tsp powdered nutmeg
- ½ tsp powdered cloves

Instructions:
1. Assemble all listed ingredients into a glass or ceramic bowl.

2. Whisk all the ingredients together thoroughly until an even, fine consistency is achieved.

3. Store the spice blend in an airtight jar.

Everything Bagel Seasoning

This incredible spice blend incorporates a variety of native and exotic spices and crushed seeds to give a simply stunning taste to a wide variety of dishes it can be used for. Due to its component elements, the seasoning is loaded with sodium and potassium, giving it considerable health benefits.

Total Cooking Time: 5 minutes

Serving Size: ¾ cup

Ingredients:

- 3 tbsp poppy seeds
- 3 tbsp sesame seeds
- 2 tbsp dried and chopped garlic
- 2 tbsp chopped and dried onions
- 3 tbsp rough salt

Instructions:

1. Heat up your sesame seeds, poppy seeds, dried garlic and onions over medium heat in a small skillet. Stir the heating mixture continuously until a distinctive smell and a light brown coloration of the spice blend is observed.

2. Pour the spice blend into a glass or ceramic bowl, add in the salt, and stir the resultant thoroughly.

3. Let the mixture cool, and then transfer to an airtight jar. The spice blend must be kept in a cool, dry place, and should preferably be stored at room temperature for not more than a month.

Sazón

This peculiarly orange spice blend casts a superb, inimitable flavor into every single dish, and with its healthy, but a strong punch of MSG (Monosodium Glutamate), it helps create truly unforgettable meals. Sazón can be used to prepare soups, stews, braises, and the seasoning of different meat products – chicken, ham, lamb, and even fish. The tangy spice blend contains a healthy dose of sodium and potassium for the proper functioning of the body.

Total Cooking Time: 3 minutes

Total Serving Size: ½ cup
Ingredients:

- 1 tbsp powdered garlic
- 1 tbsp onion powder
- 1 tbsp grounded cumin
- 1 tbsp powdered turmeric
- ½ tbsp ground black pepper
- 2 tbsp salt
- 2 tbsp sweet paprika

Instructions:

1. Add all listed ingredients into a bowl and whisk thoroughly until an even, homogenous mixture is attained.

2. Transfer the spice blend into an airtight bowl, and store in a cool, dark and dry place.

Montreal Steak Spice Mix

This vintage spice blend is a true classic, and it promises to add a taste of antique excitement to every meal you use it for. Making the Montreal Steak spice mix in the comfort of your home is quite fun, and it also helps you to save money.

The Montreal Steak spice mix can be used as a rub for all types of steak, chicken, and fish.

Total Cooking Time: 10 minutes
Serving Size: ½ cup
Ingredients:

- 2 tbsp black peppercorns
- 1 tbsp mustard seeds
- 2 tsp dill seeds
- 1 tsp coriander seeds
- 1 tbsp + 1 tsp kosher salt
- 1 tbsp + 1 tsp dried and chopped garlic
- 1 tsp crushed red pepper flakes

Instructions:

1. In a small skillet, heat the peppercorns, mustard seeds, dill seeds, and coriander seeds at medium heat.

2. Stir the mixture in the skillet continuously until a distinctive aroma is detected. The seeds should begin to pop after 2 minutes.

3. Pour the gritty mixture into a mortar and crush further with a pestle.

4. Add in your salt, garlic, and chili grits, and crush all ingredients until your desired consistency is achieved.

5. Transfer the mixture into an airtight jar, keep in a cool, dry place, and use within a month of preparation.

Crudités with Chile Lime Salt

This exotic spice blend helps to add a touch of tangy zest to every single dish. This mix is, however, mostly used as a dip for raw fruits and vegetables. With the Crudites with Lime Salt spice mix, eating healthy becomes a whole new adventure. The spice mix packs a healthy punch of sodium and potassium, giving it tremendous health benefits.

Total Cooking Time: 30 minutes

Serving Size: 8 – 10 servings

Ingredients:

- 1 lime
- 2 tbsp coarse sea salt
- ½ tsp ancho chile powder
- 2 oranges
- 5 small, seedless cucumbers
- 1 bunch of radishes
- large jigama

Instructions:

1. Cut up your oranges into small 1/4 inch rounds and cut

up each round in half.

2. Cut your cucumber into ½ inch bits

3. Cut up all radishes in halves.

4. Peel the jigama, cut it into ¼-inch thick slices. Then further cut half the slices into semi-circles, and the other slices into triangles.

5. Peel your lime and process the lime zest into a small bowl. Add in your salt and chili powder into the bowl and stir thoroughly.

6. Cut the lime into wedges and arrange all other ingredients on a platter. Squeeze the lime juice onto the assortment of ingredients and sprinkle in the spiced salt mixture.

7. Serve the spice mix alongside the remaining spice salt.

Ras-El-Hanout

This vibrant and versatile spice mix has its origin in the dry plains of Morocco in North Africa. Apart from its deep cultural roots, the Ras-El-Hanout is also famous for the irresistible taste it brings to every single dish. It is commonly used in the preparation of roast chicken or grilled lamb. This pulsating spice blend needs to keep in a cool and dry environment at all times to preserve its quality.

Total Cooking Time: 5 minutes

Serving Size: 2 tbsp

Ingredients:

- 1 tsp cumin
- 1 tsp ground ginger
- ¾ tsp ground black pepper
- ¼ tsp ground cloves
- ½ tsp ground coriander
- 1 tsp salt
- ½ tsp powdered cayenne pepper
- ½ tsp powdered cinnamon
- ½ tsp ground allspice

Instructions:

1. Get your ceramic bowl or anything similar and pour the ingredients into the base.

2. Mix gently but consistently until you get a fine blend.

3. Now, transfer the content to an airtight container. Always keep covered.

Lebkuchen Spice Mix

This brilliant spice mix has its origins in Europe – Germany, to be precise. It is famous for the pumpkin pie spice mix and can be used for virtually everything the pumpkin pie spice mix can be used for. The Lebkuchen spice mix is highly revered in its native Germany, its mostly only sold around Christmas in local stores for use in baking Christmas pastries. As soon as the Yuletide passes, the gorgeous bottles of Lebkuchen are kept again, only to be seen again on another Christmas.

Lebkuchen spice mix is widely used to give cinnamon rolls, and glazed apple cakes their uniquely irresistible tastes. Each ingredient that makes up this spice blend can be altered in quantity to give just the right, desired flavor.

Cooking Time: 5 minutes

Serving Size: ½ cup

Ingredients:

- 5 tbsp. ground cinnamon
- 1½ tbsp ground cloves
- 1 tsp ground allspice
- 1 tsp ground mace
- ¾ tsp crushed aniseed

Instructions:

1. Gather all the ingredients and dump them into a bowl.

2. Mix with a ladle or anything utensil until you get a fine consistency.

3. Remove the mixture from the bowl and transfer to an airtight container. Keep away from moisture and direct sunlight.

4. This resilient spice can retain its distinct flavor for up to one year.

Sriracha Salt

This amazing blend was invented in the early 20th century in Thailand but didn't find its way into the US market until the 1980s. Fortunately, this spice was definitely worth the wait because of its incredible flavor and its unrivalled versatility. The Sriracha salt blend can be used to spice up just about anything – popcorn, noodles, fried potatoes, and even fruits and veggies.

Total Cooking Time: 24 hours

Serving Size: 1 cup.

Ingredients:

- 2 tbsp sriracha sauce
- 1 cup unrefined sea salt

Instructions:

1. Stir the salt and the sauce thoroughly until an even mixture is achieved.

2. Spread the mixture on a dry baking sheet, and place in

an oven set to 100°F overnight.

3. Remove the dried mixture from the oven and crush the lumps with a spoon until a fine consistency is attained.

4. Store the blend in an airtight jar and keep away from moisture.

Tandoori Spice Blend

This brightly colored spice mix packs a unique tangy taste, a stunning flavor, and can be used for a wide range of foods. It is, however, popularly used as a rub for different meat types – chicken, beef, ham, and sometimes, fish.

Cooking Time: 5 minutes

Serving Size: 2 tbsp + 1 tsp

Ingredients:

- 1 tsp ground ginger
- 1 tsp ground cayenne pepper
- 1 tsp ground cumin
- 1 tsp powdered coriander
- 1 tsp ground turmeric
- 1 tsp paprika

- 1 tsp table salt

Instructions:

1. Find a bowl, put all the ingredients into it, and mix gently but consistently until you get a fine blend.

2. Transfer the even mixture into an airtight jar and use within two weeks of preparation.

Creole Seasoning

This vintage spice mix offers an amazing flavor and unrivalled flexibility. The Creole seasoning mix can be used for a variety of foods – stews, soups, and shrimp, and also functions as a superb meat rub.

Total Cooking Time: 5 minutes
Total Serving Size: 1 cup
Ingredients:

- 1/3 CUP paprika
- 3 tbsp ground black pepper
- 3 tbsp dried oregano
- 2 tbsp Kosher salt

- 2 tbsp dried basil
- 1 tbsp dried powdered onions
- 1 tbsp ground cayenne pepper
- 4 tsp ground garlic
- 4 tsp dried thyme

Instructions:

1. Assemble all collected ingredients in a bowl and mix thoroughly until an even, fine consistency is achieved.

2. Transfer the mixture into an airtight jar and store for a maximum of 3 months.

Dry Chimichurri Rub

This scintillating spice mix has its origins in the South American plains of Argentina. It is usually combined with oil and vinegar to create an irresistible rub for different meat types ranging from grilled chicken to beef and ham. To get the most spectacular results out of this blend, dried herb leaves are recommended instead of processed herbs.

Total Cooking Time: 10 minutes

Total Serving Size: ¾ cup

Ingredients:

- 3 tbsp dried basil leaves
- 3 tbsp dried oregano leaves
- 1 tbsp ground black pepper
- 2 tsp garlic powder
- 1 tbsp dried savory leaves
- 2 tsp dried grounded pepper
- 2 tbsp dried parsley flakes
- 2 tbsp dried parsley leaves
- 2 tbsp dried thyme leaves
- 2 tbsp coarse Kosher salt
- 1 tbsp smoked paprika

Instructions:

1. All spices should be assembled in a grease-free glass or ceramic bowl and mixed thoroughly until a consistent mixture is achieved.

2. The mixture can be stored in an airtight jar. It must be used within one month of preparation.

Fette Sau Dry Rub

The Fette Sau dry rub is a simple, yet utterly delightful spice blend that has been in use for decades as a rub for all meat types. The unique spice blend confers an exquisite and exotic flavor to every food it is used for. All ingredient amounts can be altered to give the perfect, desired taste.

Total Cooking Time: 5 minutes

Serving Size: 4 cups

Ingredients:

- 1 cup Kosher salt
- 1½ cups dark brown sugar
- 1 cup ground espresso beans
- ¼ cup ground garlic
- ¼ cup ground black pepper
- 2 tbsp ground cinnamon
- 2 tbsp powdered cumin
- 2 tbsp cayenne pepper

Instructions:

1. Gather all ingredients and add them into a bowl and whisk thoroughly until a fine and even consistency is achieved.

2. The spice mix should then be transferred into an airtight jar and stored in a cool, dry place.

CONCLUSION

You have finally made it to the end of this book, and if you have practiced every single recipe along the way as you read, I say to you: "Kudos!" If you have simply just read through to get a feel of the spice mixes mentioned, well, congratulations, now you have learned about the wonders of home-made spice mixes. However, this experience cannot be complete without you actually getting down to the business of preparing each spice mix and using it to prepare your favorite meal.

Therefore, this might be the end of this book, but it definitely is not the end of your learning process. The explicit instructions in each recipe will always be here to guide you every time you want to try out a new blend, and the taste of delight on your taste buds as you savor the results of your dedication promises to remain forever unforgettable.

So, thank you for reading this book, and congratulations

once again on completing it and giving your culinary knowledge a boost. Now, practice till you get perfect, and keep creating meals that would make for experiences of a lifetime. Welcome, once again, to a world filled with infinite flavors!